There Will Be Some Slight Interference

A ~~Half-Baked~~ One-Act Play by Patrick Blosse

DiaBlo Publishing

Published by DiaBlo Publishing, 2024

ISBN: 9798882178023

First edition

Printed by Kindle Direct Publishing in the United Kingdom

Other books by Pat Blosse:

Novels and Short Stories

The Red Bonnet (a supernatural mystery thriller)

Short and Sweet: 100-Word Stories

Plays

Heaven's Above (one-act play for children)

In collaboration with Dennis Diamond

    The Cat Flap (three-act Agatha Christie spoof)

    The Ghosts of Martha Rudd (three-act ghostly comedy)

    Lost But Not Least (one-act Shakespearean drama)

    Sketches in Hyde Park (5-part radio play)

Contact:

patblosse@gmail.com or

on Facebook at Patrick Blosse_Author Page

Copyright © 2024, Patrick G Blosse

All Rights Reserved

The characters and events portrayed in this play are fictitious. Any similarity to real persons, living or dead, is coincidental and not intended by the author.

No part of this book may be reproduced, or stored in a retrieval system, or transmitted in any form or by any means, electronic, mechanical, photocopying, recording, or otherwise, without express written permission of the publisher.

Characters (in order of appearance)

Alvar Lidell The voice of the BBC.

Dotti Darling (*30-50*) A BBC producer. She is quite happy doing 'Listen with Mother' but can't cope with the stress of grown-up people. She drifts through life in a rather lovely haze.

Molly Proppemup (*Age indeterminable*) A BBC char lady. Easily confused with her mop, her rough and ready exterior covers hidden depths of stupidity. There may be more to her than meets the eye, but, if so, she hides it well. She wears a long housecoat and a scarf wrapped around her hair.

Simone deWitt (*40-55*) A BBC floor manager. A volunteer, this is her way of "doing her bit for the war". She would have been better employed packing parachutes (for the enemy). She is the antithesis of Dotti Darling – dashing from one crisis to another at a rate of knots. Her hair is held back in a tight bun. Simone is very close to the edge; unfortunately, she is on the wrong side of it.

Clive Prendaghast (*45-55*) An actor of some little repute. Some very little repute as it happens. His repertoire includes some of the greatest plays of all time – Hamlet (second gravedigger), Julius Caesar (spear-holder) and Macbeth (a dead body). In farce, he is always the little Yorkshireman who gets locked in a trunk and loses his trousers. His idea of hell is to be forced to perform with amateurs he has never met in a poorly rehearsed radio play with a rotten script.

Dame Hari-Kiri te Kanawerms (*50-60*) A diva. Once Britain's leading opera singer, she has appeared at every great venue in the Western world. The war has now reduced her to entertaining the 'boys' from the back of troop carriers. She would give her life for music and a little gin and lime.

Celia Stringbag (*60-ish*) Dresser and permanent companion to the diva. She has never been known to open her mouth in public but her looks speak volumes (usually daggers).

Rev. Reginald Cadwallader-Trump (*70-ish*) The shambling vicar of All-Hallows. He should have been retired years ago but all the young men are at 'the front'. He has turned up to do 'The

	Epilogue'. Not at home with new-fangled things like wireless sets. In fact, barely at home at all about anything. Tall, thin, slightly stooped.
Willie Nobbs	(*11-14*) An East-End urchin evacuated to live with Dame Hari-Kiri. He will grow up to take part in the Great Train Robbery but, for now, must content himself with petty pilfering and passing secrets to the Germans. He only ever gets one thing wrong. He gets caught. He wears a drab, grey school uniform with short trousers and a cap. Both of his socks are rolled own.
Dickie 'the Dip' Nobbs	(*13-16*) Willie's elder, and much wiser brother. Looks like a choir boy and could charm the birds from the trees. Old ladies love him. Runs a black market in watches, nylons and sausages. Will grow up to head a multi-billion pound pubs and gambling consortium and advise the government on foreign investment. Wears the same grey school uniform as Willie but his is cleaner and tidier and his sock are neatly held up with school-issue garters.

Verity Pureheart (*18-20*) A young, sweet-natured Wren, on leave from her posting in Portsmouth and hoping to meet her heart-throb, Ronald Coleman. Wears a Wren's uniform with beret-style cap with an 'HMS' cap-band. She has a 'modern' hairstyle, similar to Mary Martin's at the time.

F X Mann (*Age immaterial*) A sound technician of unsound mind

Miss/Mr Phillimore (*Any age or gender*) A passing pianist

Aladdin A Brown Serge Suit

During the action, our cast puts on a radio play entitled 'Aladdin A Brown Serge Suit' or 'It's Behind You, Mr. Hitler' – with the following cast:

Private Aladdin, a raw recruit to the British Army
Verity Pureheart

Sergeant Major Balthazar, his worst enemy
Rev. Reginald Cadwallader-Trump

Widow Twankey, manageress of the NAAFI, Aladdin's Aunt
Dame Hari-Kiri te Kanawerms

Privates Wishy and Washy, Aladdin's cousins
Willie and Dickie Nobbs

A Genie With Light Brown Hair, and everyone else
Clive Prendaghast

The Setting

The play is set in a small radio studio in the bowels of Broadcasting House, at a not very secret location somewhere in London, England. It is Christmas 1942.

A glass screen L gives a dim view of the producer's 'box' next door. A sign above the screen lights up to display 'ON AIR' in large red letters when appropriate. A door DL leads into the producer's box and all other parts of the building. A sparse Christmas tree, with an old and tatty fairy precariously balanced on top, stands UL on a small table. It supports a handful of drab looking, home-made decorations. Somebody has drawn a 'Chad' on a piece of 'festive' card pinned to the table. It bears the legend "Wot – no presents?"

A large counter stands UR. Underneath it, unseen as yet, is a variety of sound effect paraphernalia including, a grit tray, boots on sticks, a bottle with a cork in it, a pane of glass and a chamois leather, a salad spinner, various bells and whistles, a duck call, a washboard, a football rattle, a bucketful of glass, a tin tray, cups, saucers, spoons and a small 'door' in a frame with various locks, bolts and bells on it. A thunder sheet is suspended behind the counter. A large, old-fashioned microphone is suspended above the counter. A small, folding card table is propped in front of the counter – as yet unopened.

Two, free-standing microphones bearing the legend 'BBC' stand downstage. A large loudspeaker is suspended high on the wall UC from which we hear occasional instructions (and other things) from the producer's box. A profusion of cables is suspended around the walls, from which hang a few limp Christmas cards.

A small, upright piano stands against the wall DR.

The Action

It is Christmas 1942. The tide of the war is changing. Only two months previously Rommel was defeated at El Alamein and now the Germans are being pushed backwards all along the Russian Front. But the blackouts, the rationing and the bleakest winter in living memory still cast a pall over the country. In his infinite and unfathomable wisdom, the Director General of the BBC has decreed that a festive pantomime on the wireless is exactly what the British people need to cheer them up......

The Play

LIGHTING FX: *The play opens in* BLACKOUT *except for the* ON AIR *light which is on*

SOUND FX: *Fade in 'Who Do You Think You Are Kidding, Mr. Hitler' (about 15 seconds and then fades out during the following speech)*

ALVAR LIDELL: (*voiceover, best BBC Received Pronunciation*) ...a big fat one right where Jerry doesn't want it. Mr. Churchill went on to say that he saw no immediate end to hostilities, but he was sure the British people had the stomach for anything the enemy had yet to throw at them. He went on to wish the House a merry and peaceful Christmas and a happy New Year. (*pause*) That is the end of the six o'clock news from the BBC on this, 24th December 1942, and this was Alvar Lidell reading it. I too wish you the compliments of the season. (*pause*) The next news headlines will be at 7 o'clock. Meanwhile, on the Light Programme, there will shortly be a new programme to the airwaves – a quiz hosted by the BBC's newest young man about town, Eamon Andrews, entitled 'What's My Line?'. Here, on the

Home Service, we will continue with a short programme of music before tonight's special production – a seasonal play entitled 'Aladdin a Brown Serge Suit' or 'It's Behind You, Mr. Hitler'.

SOUND FX: *Fade in Glenn Miller's* Tuxedo Junction (*softly*)

LIGHTING FX: *The* ON AIR *light goes off*

DOTTI DARLING: (*over loudspeaker – gushing*) ...thank you, Alvar, my darling. That was lovely – gorgeous. Just the right tone. Serious but straightforward with the merest hint of seasonal frivolity. Perfect.

LIGHTING FX: *Lights spring on to reveal a shabby radio studio.*

The door DL is just being slammed shut. We see the back view of a man in evening dress and tails as he exits. The door swings open - slightly ajar.

ALVAR LIDELL: (*off L, his plummy, radio announcer's voice has disappeared*)   Naff off!

DOTTI DARLING: (*voiceover*)   Oh, I say!

ALVAR LIDELL: (*off L*)   And turn that blasted row off!

DOTTI DARLING: (*voiceover*)   Ouch!

SOUND FX: Tuxedo Junction *stops abruptly with a squawk. We are now able to hear all that is going on in the producer's box over the loudspeaker.*

The door DL opens and MOLLY PROPPEMUP, *a cleaning lady of no fixed appearance wanders in dragging a mop behind her. During the next few lines she props her mop against the counter, takes out a duster and meticulously dusts the counter, microphones and Christmas decorations, using her sleeve for extra polishing power. She seems to take pride in her work, examining everything minutely, especially the Christmas cards, occasionally making notes in a small notebook. We can follow the highs and lows of the argument going on in the producer's box through her reactions and expressions.*

DOTTI DARLING: (*over loudspeaker*) Do you mind? That hurt! I was about to wish you a merry Christmas but clearly you are already drunk, so I shan't bother.

ALVAR LIDELL: (*over loudspeaker*) Madam, I don't give a damn!

DOTTI DARLING: (*over loudspeaker*) You've been watching 'Gone with the Wind' again, haven't you? You're getting a Rhet Butler complex. You will have to sober up soon; you've got to read the news again at 7 o'clock. (*pause*) And my name is not 'Madam'. It's Dotti. Dotti Darling -

to my friends. Not that you're my friend at the moment.

ALVAR LIDELL: (*over loudspeaker*)　　Madam, I don't...

DOTTI DARLING: (*over loudspeaker*)　　...give a damn? Oh, do go and lie down, Alvar, there's a good boy.

ALVAR LIDELL: (*over loudspeaker*)　　And don't talk to me like I'm a 6-year-old.

DOTTI DARLING: (*over loudspeaker*)　　Then don't behave like one. I really don't know why you have to drink so much. The Director General will have your guts for garters when he finds out.

SOUND FX:　　*A DOOR OPENS hurriedly at the back of the auditorium. Simone deWitt rushes down to the stage, looking very agitated*

ALVAR LIDELL: (*over loudspeaker*)　　The Director General can talk a long walk off a short...*hic*

DOTTI DARLING: (*over loudspeaker*)　　...pier?

ALVAR LIDELL: (*over loudspeaker*)　　...for all I care. I just don't give a....*hic*

DOTTI DARLING: (*over loudspeaker*)　　...damn.

ALVAR LIDELL: (*over loudspeaker*)　　Thank you.

SIMONE deWITT: (*reaching the door DL, panting for breath*) Are they here yet?

DOTTI DARLING: (*over loudspeaker*) Who?

SIMONE deWITT: (*at door, panicking*) The cast – the actors – the Great Northern Theatre Company of Bridlingham-by-the-Sea (*or insert your own local amateur group!*) – the 'Aladdin A Brown Serge Suit' brigade – the very nub of our existence on this earth tonight! (exits DL, closing the door behind her)

DOTTI DARLING: (*over loudspeaker*) Haven't seen them, love. I'm only the producer. What do I know? What do they look like?

SIMONE deWITT: (*over loudspeaker, her voice rising another semi-tone*) How should I know?

ALVAR LIDELL: (*over loudspeaker*) They're easy to spot, Simone. Flat caps, whippets and a terrible whiff of greasepaint. (*or add you own local colour*)

SIMONE deWITT: (*over loudspeaker*) You're no help at all.

DOTTI DARLING: (*over loudspeaker*) He's drunk.

MOLLY PROPPEMUP tries to peer through the keyhole of the door DL but gives up after a couple of lines when she can't see anything.

SIMONE deWITT: (*over loudspeaker*)   What are we going to do?!

DOTTI DARLING: (*over loudspeaker*)   We could try black coffee and a walk in the fresh air.

SIMONE deWITT: (*over loudspeaker*)   Not him, you brainless idiot. How are we going to find a cast for tonight's pantomime? It's going out live in 15 minutes!

DOTTI DARLING: (*over loudspeaker*)   That's a bit of a teaser, isn't it?

ALVAR LIDELL: (*over loudspeaker*)   They'll be on one of those trains stuck in Crewe. (*or a more local station*) Leaves on the line. I announced it on the 6 o'clock news.

SIMONE deWITT: (*over loudspeaker, screeching*)
Well, why didn't you say so before?!

ALVAR LIDELL: (*over loudspeaker*)   (*screeches*) I did! (*pause, normal voice*) At 6 o'clock. I don't know why I bother to read the news; nobody ever listens to a bloody word I say. I might just as well talk to myself for all the notice anyone takes.

SIMONE deWITT: (*over loudspeaker*)   Did you speak? I'm thinking.

ALVAR LIDELL: (*over loudspeaker*)   I said, I might just as well talk to myself for all the notice….. Well, there you are, you see. You weren't listening!

MOLLY *PROPPEMUP takes a large apple from her pocket, dusts it, huffs on it, polishes it on her sleeve and takes a large bite.*

ALVAR LIDELL: (*continuing, over loudspeaker*)   …I sit here every day, dressed to the nines, droning on to thousands of people up and down the country, people I never meet, telling them things they don't want to hear. Bad news piled upon more bad news. If it's not the German Army advancing, it's the pound dropping or more rationing – or leaves on the line at Crewe. Is it any wonder I turn to drink, I ask myself? No, it's not, I say, because no-one's ever bloody listening to me…..

SIMONE deWITT: (*over loudspeaker*)   Belt up, Alvar. I'm concentrating. Dotti. You go upstairs and see if you can find anyone wandering about in the lobby. Actors, cleaners, camera crew, visitors – it doesn't matter. Deaf, mad or blind – tonight they're going to be radio stars. There's a studio audience next door waiting for that new show 'What's My Line'. I'll go and round up some of them.

The door DL opens abruptly. SIMONE deWITT *enters in a hurry. She is dressed in tweeds, carries a clipboard and has a large pair of earphones around her neck.* MOLLY PROPPEMUP *quietly exits DL, doing her best to slide away behind* SIMONE *and not be seen.* SIMONE *does not register her.*

LIGHTING FX: HOUSE LIGHTS COME UP

SIMONE deWITT: (*addressing the audience, suddenly cool, calm and collected*)   Good evening, Ladies and Gentlemen. My name is Simone deWitt. I'm what we call a Floor Manager here at the BBC. I'm sorry to say we have a very slight technical issue with the studio next door. I know you're all here to see 'What's My Line' but I wonder, is there anyone in the house with some – well, um, some acting talent? A school play perhaps or maybe a little public speaking experience? We wouldn't be asking you to do anything terribly

	complicated or – or anything, but we need some – er, we need some….one.
CLIVE PRENDAGHAST:	(*standing up at the rear of the hall*)
	I say. I'm an actor.
SIMONE deWITT:	Oh, thank God for that. I mean, that's wonderful –
CLIVE PRENDAGHAST:	You may have heard of me. (*looking around him, clearly expecting a round of applause*) Clive Prendaghast.
SIMONE deWITT:	Sorry – no.
CLIVE PRENDAGHAST:	Hamlet – Stratford – 1938.
SIMONE deWITT:	You were Hamlet?
CLIVE PRENDAGHAST:	Second Gravedigger.
SIMONE deWITT:	Well, never mind.
CLIVE PRENDAGHAST:	(*moving down through the audience to join* SIMONE *and pulling a much-thumbed newspaper cutting from his pocket*) My performance was much acclaimed in the North Devon Journal. (*or similar local newspaper*) Look. (*in loud, ringing tones*) "Mrs. Prendaghast's performance"...I think that's just a typographical

error…"<u>Mr.</u> Prendaghast's performance as the second gravedigger could not be missed…"

SIMONE deWITT: I'm sure you were lovely but we don't have time…

CLIVE PRENDAGHAST: (*spotting a 'celebrity' in the front row*) Why, it's Dame Hari-Kiri isn't it?

DAME HARI-KIRI DE KANAWERMS *squirms in her seat, not wanting to be recognized.*

CLIVE PRENDAGHAST: (*thick skinned*) Yes, it is! Dame Hari-Kiri de Kanawerms, if I live and breathe. Well we haven't met in….

DAME HARI-KIRI: (*severely*) Ever.

CLIVE: Years. When was it? The Palladium, 1932?

DAME HARI-KIRI: I think you must be mistaken.

CLIVE: No, it was that charity bash at The Coliseum. Do you remember? You spilled your gin and lime all over the Peruvian Ambassador's wife. Frightful mess. Nearly caused a small war, I remember. I say, you weren't in Poland in 1939 by any chance…?

DAME HARI-KIRI: Really!

CLIVE: Sorry. Poor taste.

SIMONE: (*much impressed*) Dame Hari-Kiri de Kanawerms? The opera singer?

DAME HARI-KIRI: Well —

SIMONE: You'd be perfect. We desperately need a dame with a good singing voice.

DAME HARI-KIRI: I really don't think…

SIMONE: You see, we have to put on this special Christmas play and the cast is stuck in Crewe and it's awfully important. A bit like a Royal Command performance if you like, and — well — we need you. We can offer you — refreshments.

DAME HARI-KIRI: Well, if you put it like that.

SIMONE: Wonderful, wonderful. We'll be eternally grateful. Wonderful.

CLIVE: Wonderful.

SIMONE: This way. There's no time to lose. (*she heads for the exit DL*)

DAME HARI-KIRI: There is one thing. I must have my dresser.

SIMONE; There's no room for furniture.

DAME HARI-KIRI: My personal dresser. (*indicates* CELIA STRINGBAG *who was sitting next to her in the front row*) This is Celia – Celia Stringbag, my personal dresser and treasured companion. She travels with me everywhere. I'd be hopelessly lost without her.

CELIA *rises.* SIMONE, *who has returned downstage, extends a hand to shake with* CELIA *but* CELIA *curtsies.*

DAME HARI-KIRI: Just a little eccentric as you can see but she's perfectly harmless. Deaf as a post, of course, poor old thing – and dumb.

CLIVE: A mute?

DAME HARI-KIRI: Can't sing a note. I mean – can't utter a word – a sound. (*to* CELIA) Can you my dear? (CELIA *opens her mouth as if to reply and* DAME HARI-KIRI *quickly covers it with her hand*) And delusions – suffers from terrible delusions. She's past it really but she's been with me so long now it would be a crime to let her go.

SIMONE: That's lovely, but really, we have no time to lose. Follow me. (*she turns and heads quickly for the door DL*)

DAME HARI-KIRI: But, my boys? Where are my boys?!

SIMONE: (*exiting DL*) No time for that now!

CLIVE: (*with a dramatic gesture*) Come, we must go. The show must go on! (*exits DL full of purpose*)

DAME HARI-KIRI: Celia – my bag

CELIA *picks up* DAME HARI-KIRI's *handbag as well as her own bag, the Dame's fox fur, her own coat and an umbrella.*

DAME HARI-KIRI: (*imperiously*) Where is my fox fur?

CELIA *puts down all the things she has just picked up, drape's the fox fur over* DAME HARI-KIRI's *shoulders, picks up everything else again and staggers off DL, following behind* DAME HARI-KIRI – *looking daggers. She kicks the door shut behind her with her foot*

LIGHTING FX:	LIGHTS DIM TO BLACKOUT
SOUND FX:	Tuxedo Junction *is heard coming to an end over the loudspeaker at very low volume.*
LIGHTING FX:	*Lights* FADE UP *onto an empty stage*
SOUND FX:	*The music continues with Glenn Miller's* Elmer's Tune *softly throughout the following scene*

A small boy's head rises slowly from behind the counter UR. It is little WILLIE NOBBS. *He looks about furtively.*

SOUND FX: *We hear a* DOOR OPENING *somewhere off L*

WILLIE NOBBS *ducks down behind the counter*

DOTTI DARLING: (*off L*) This way, Reverend. This way. It's very good of you to volunteer.

REV. REGINALD CADWALLADER-TRUMP: (*off L*)

Through here? (*the door DL opens half way*)

DOTTI DARLING: (*off L*) No, that's the studio. We won't go in there just yet. Come through to my office and I'll explain our problem. (*the door DL closes*)

SOUND FX: *We hear a* DOOR CLOSE *somewhere off L*

After a few seconds, WILLIE NOBBS' head appears above the counter again – slowly. He looks about furtively as he had done before.

DICKIE 'THE DIP' NOBBS: (*popping up from behind the counter, next to* WILLIE) Oh, I'm fed up with this. There's no Germans round 'ere. (*he moves round to the front of the counter*)

WILLIE NOBBS: (*rising*) 'Course there is, Dickie. You just gotta wait. You gotta be patient, see. Your Jerry, he doesn't go advertising what e's going to do, does 'e? 'e doesn't put an advert in the paper sayin' "I will be invading London on Thursday night – bring a bottle", does 'e? No – e's suttle. 'e 'angs about in likely places, lookin' for fifth columnists and Bolsheviks and double agents and the like so as 'e can pick up any secrets wot 'appens to fall out of people's pockets.

DICKIE: So what are we doin' 'ere then?

WILLIE: (*moving round to the front of the counter*) This is the BBC innit? This is where they all come from.

DICKIE: Who?

WILLIE: The fifth columnists, of course. It's a well-known fact. Cambridge University, the House of Lords and the BBC – they're all hotbeds of – of – somethin'.

DICKIE: Well, you're so clever, Willie Nobbs, where are they then? We've bin 'ere for nearly 'alf an hour and I haven't seen a single double agent or fifth columnist – let alone a German. I reckon there's no future in trying to catch Germans. We

	should stick to what we know. Let's go and hawk a few nylons instead.
SOUND FX:	*We hear the sound of a* DOOR OPENING *somewhere off L.* ELMER'S TUNE FADES OUT
SIMONE: (*off L*)	This way. Chop, chop. No time to dawdle. Follow me.
WILLIE:	Look out. We got trouble.
DICKIE:	Come on. We'll get out this way. Nobody'll see us.

WILLIE *and* DICKIE *walk quickly down through the audience to the back of the hall and sit on two spare chairs in the back row.*

LIGHTING FX:	*The lights dim to* BLACKOUT
DICKIE: (*at the back of the hall*)	'ere – is this the audience for 'What's My Line'?
WILLIE: (*at the back of the hall*)	I dunno. Why?
DICKIE:	(*at the back of the hall*) Isn't this where we left the Dame?
WILLIE:	(*at the back of the hall*) What, old tin drawers? We're best shot of 'er.
LIGHTING FX:	The LIGHTS COME UP on an empty stage.

MOLLY PROPPEMUP *enters DL, dragging her mop morosely behind her. During the following speeches she takes a sandwich from her pocket, unwraps it from its greaseproof paper and bites into it. Her actions are slow and deliberate.*

DICKIE: *(leaning forward and tapping the shoulder of someone in the audience in the row in front of him)* 'Ere, lady. Wanna buy some nylons – cheap?

The door DL opens quickly and SIMONE deWITT *enters in a rush.*

SIMONE: (*she moves DR, speaking clearly and studying her clipboard while addressing the people who she assumes have entered behind her – but they haven't*) ...and really, that's all there is to it. You have your scripts. All you need to do is say the words – in the right order if you can – and our team of technicians will do the rest. The 'on air' light will come on when we're broadcasting but apart from that you can speak freely. So – (*she turns around to address the 'cast', looking down at her clipboard*) – speak clearly, keep your scripts quiet, no sniggering when someone else is talking. We have eight minutes before we're on the air. Good luck. (*She looks up* *and suddenly realises that the only cast she is addressing is* MOLLY PROPPEMUP *who is leaning on her mop and chewing her sandwich*) Aaaargh! (*she rushes off DL*)

MOLLY PROPPEMUP *puts what is left of her sandwich in her pocket and starts mopping the floor.*

LIGHTING FX: The lights dim ALMOST TO BLACKOUT

WILLIE: (*at the back of the hall, after a short pause*) Nothin's 'appening'.

DICKIE: (*at the back of the hall*) Let's scarper.

The two boys move down through the audience to the stage. They are looking about them, bent on more mischief, when the door DL opens sharply.

LIGHTING FX: The stage lights come on quickly.

The two BOYS *are caught frozen in a 'stealthy' pose.* MOLLY PROPPEMUP *is peering into the piano DR with a torch. She quickly closes the lid of the piano, hides the torch before anyone notices, and carries on mopping.* DOTTI DARLING *enters as the lights come on, followed by* CLIVE PRENDAGHAST, DAME HARI-KIRI, CELIA STRINGBAG *and* REVEREND CADWALLADER-TRUMP. *The* REVEREND *is wearing a dog-collar and, although it is a bleak mid-winter's evening, he is dressed in light cotton trousers and jacket and a Panama hat – more suitable for a summer fete. He has a slight stoop and carries a script.* CLIVE PRENDAGHAST *carries a script, which he is studying closely, and a battered old Gladstone bag.* CELIA *carries her own and the* DAME's *handbags and the umbrella.* DAME HARI-KIRI *is wearing her fox fur and carries only a script.* DOTTI *carries a clipboard and three spare scripts.*

DOTTI: Hello, what are you two boys doing here? (*the boys try to get away but she catches one of them by the ear*) Never mind. We need all the help we can get. Can you read?

DAME HARI-KIRI: My little darlings!

DOTTI: Do you know these boys?

DAME HARI-KIRI: They are my evacuees. Such poor, deprived little darlings. Oh, come here my sweeties. (*she hugs them close. The* BOYS *do their best to escape but to no avail*) Where have you been? Were you lost? Oh, you must have been terrified. Poor darlings (*she smothers their delicate little ears*) Moved out from the East End, you know. Broken homes I shouldn't wonder. (*releases her hold on them a little*) But hearts of gold! (*she tries to give* DICKIE *a big kiss*)

DICKIE: (*struggling free*) Get off, yer daft bat!

DOTTI:	Very moving, I'm sure. (*she thrusts scripts into the two* BOYS' *hands*) Take these. Your parts are marked. WISHY and WASHY. Just make the best of it – and no larking about. Now – where's the floor manager? (*calls out*) Simone!! She's never here when you want her.

WILLIE *and* DICKIE *go off into a corner with their scripts and avidly search through them. We occasionally hear little sniggers and giggles from them.*

REVEREND:	Er – I say. I think there must have been some mistake.
DOTTI:	There's no doubt about that, my love.
REVEREND:	You see, I don't think this is my script
DOTTI:	What have you got? (*she takes his script and thumbs through it*) Balthazar, the wicked Sargent-Major. Well, you sort of look the part. (*sarcastically*) What would you rather be – the principal boy? (WILLIE *and* DICKIE *find this extremely funny*)
REVEREND:	Principal boy?

DOTTI: (*thrusting the script back at him*) Sorry, my darling. You just don't have the thighs for it.

REVEREND: I know I'm sometimes a bit behind the times, but is this really how you do it nowadays?

CLIVE: There's a war on love. You just have to take what you can get.

REVEREND: I suppose so – but it seems a strange way to present The Epilogue, if you ask me.

CLIVE, DAME HARI-KIRI, CELIA *and* MOLLY PROPPEMUP *all look at the* REVEREND *askance.*

DOTTI: You didn't listen to a word I said, did you? (*to the other three*) He thinks he's here to do The Epilogue.

REVEREND: Oh no, I'm <u>sure</u> I'm here to do The Epilogue. I'm most careful about my appointments. Look, it's here in my pocketbook. (*looking in his pockets for a diary*) Somewhere. (*he searches his jacket and trousers and a large, rolled-up document, tied in pink ribbon and sealing wax, falls from one of his capacious pockets. He gathers it up quickly and stuffs it* *back into his jacket guiltily. All the cast watch him but take no notice.)*

Meanwhile, WILLIE *and* DICKIE *creep up behind* MOLLY PROPPEMUP, *who has her back to the boys and is dusting each of the piano keys individually. They pinch her bottom and she screams just as the door DL bursts open and* SIMONE *rushes in, followed more sedately by* VERITY PUREHEART *in a Wren's uniform.*

SIMONE: They've gone! They've gone! (*spots the 'cast'*) Oh, they've come back!

VERITY *calmly takes in the scene.* MOLLY *is screeching, the* BOYS *are hopping up and down with glee, the* REVEREND *is stuffing the 'secret document' into his jacket and* CLIVE *is doing warming-up exercises for his face with accompanying funny noises.* DAME HARI-KIRI *is making some minor changes to her make-up.* MOLLY *clips both boys round the ears and they skulk back to their corner with their scripts.* CLIVE *starts pacing up and down the stage and gesticulating as if silently rehearsing a great dramatic piece.*

DOTTI: Do try to calm down, Simone. You're doing my blood pressure no good at all. Did you find a sound technician? I think we're going to need one.

SIMONE: A sound technician!! (*she rushes off DL and instantly rushes back again*) We've only got three minutes! (*she rushes off again DL*)

DOTTI: (*to* VERITY) Hello, my dear. Have you come to help?

VERITY PUREHEART: Hello, I'm Verity Pureheart. Your friend, Miss deWitt asked me to come and help you out.

DOTTI: (*stepping out of* CLIVE's *way*) You just happened along, did you?

VERITY: I'm on a 48-hour pass from Portsmouth. I – I was in the lobby....

CLIVE: (*as he passes by*) If I had 48 hours away from the war, I'd find something better to do than hang around the lobby of the BBC. (*continues pacing*) The <u>rain </u>in <u>Spain</u> falls <u>mainly</u> on the <u>plain</u>.

VERITY: It's a bit embarrassing actually. I was hoping to find – someone.

DAME HARI-KIRI: (*while trying to do her lipstick*) Ronald Coleman, I shouldn't wonder.

CLIVE, *having finished pacing up and down, goes to the counter and picks up the card table, which he erects between the two microphones and as far downstage as he can get it.*

VERITY: Yes – that's it.

DAME HARI-KIRI: Don't you worry about that, my girl. I'd be doing the same at your age. (VERITY *smiles demurely*)

DOTTI: Well, you're a little darling and no mistake. Could you slap your thigh for me?

VERITY: Slap my....?

DOTTI: Thigh.

VERITY: Well – if it's important... (*she slaps her thigh in perfect pantomime fashion*)

DOTTI: Perfect! You were born to be Aladdin. (*hands VERITY a script*) 'Aladdin a Brown Serge Suit'. Start at page one and just do your best. We're on in less than two minutes.

CLIVE: (*to DOTTI*) Excuse me, but I don't seem to have been allotted my part.

DOTTI: Oh, didn't you realise?

CLIVE: (*indicating his script*) Someone's written here on the front 'E-E' but there isn't a part with the initials E-E.

DOTTI: But my darling, that just means 'everyone else'.

CLIVE: Oh. What?! Everyone else – you mean – *everyone* else?

DOTTI: Yes, darling. Well, you are the only real actor. You should be able to manage that – shouldn't you?

CLIVE: Oh, well – I suppose... At least, I've got my hats. (*he picks up his Gladstone bag and puts it on the card table*)

DOTTI: (*not understanding what he means*) Good.

CLIVE: (*opening his Gladstone bag, he takes out one or two hats and tries them on*) You see, the art of good acting starts with the headgear. If you can work out what your character would wear on his head, that's half the battle won. (*he dons a Napoleon hat and a stance and voice to fit*) Not tonight, Josephine.

The door DL bursts open and SIMONE enters, dishevelled and breathless.

SIMONE: (*to DOTTI*) No luck – no technicians – all gone home – Christmas shopping.

DOTTI: Then find someone else, darling. I'll be in my box. (*to the 'cast'*) Break a leg everybody. (DOTTI *exits DL saying*) Ninety seconds left!

SIMONE:	Ninety seconds! (SIMONE *faints under the strain, into the arms of* CLIVE)
CLIVE:	She's fainted.
DAME HARI-KIRI:	So I see.
CLIVE:	What shall we do?
DAME HARI-KIRI:	Well, I don't know about you but I'm going to breathe a sigh of relief.
REVEREND:	I may have some smelling salts here. (*he searches his pockets. The 'pink ribbon and sealing wax' document comes out again and is hurriedly put into a back trouser pocket where it can be clearly seen poking out from under his jacket*)

MOLLY *sees the 'secret document' and takes an intense interest in it. During the following few speeches she creeps up behind the* REVEREND *and tries to pull the document out without anyone seeing her.*

CLIVE:	I'm not worried about her. What are we going to do without an effects man?
VERITY:	Never fear. Keep a cool head. (*into microphone*) Dotti, can you hear me?
DOTTI: (*over loudspeaker*)	Clear as a bell, Verity.

VERITY: (*into microphone*) Turn the house lights on, please. There must be someone in the audience who can help.

LIGHTING FX: The HOUSE LIGHT *come on*

MOLLY *is just making a grab for the* REVEREND's *rear end when the house lights come on. This startles the* REVEREND, *who takes step backwards.* MOLLY PROPPEMUP *is left poised in mid-air, leaning forward with one arm out-stretched. She tries to continue the move by turning it into a pirouette, then arabesques across the stage and exits DL.*

REVEREND: My goodness. I didn't realise there were so many people watching us.

CLIVE: What shall I do with this? (*indicating* SIMONE, *who he is still supporting*)

DAME HARI-KIRI: Celia!

CELIA *puts down her bags and umbrella, takes* SIMONE *from* CLIVE *and drags her off DL. (If she is strong enough, she could throw her over her shoulder to carry her off.)*

DAME HARI-KIRI: You see. She has her uses.

CLIVE: I say, isn't that the same lot who were watching What's My Line?

DAME HARI-KIRI: (*studying the first row closely*) No, they were much better looking than this lot.

VERITY: (*to audience after slight pause*) Is there an effects man in the audience?

F X MANN: (*standing up at back of the hall*) Here.

DAME HARI-KIRI: You are an effects man – a sound technician?

F X MANN: Oh no – I'm F X Mann – that is Fiona Xavier Mann (*pause*) two Ns

DAME HAR-KIRI: You'll do.

DOTTI: (*over loudspeaker*) Sorry to break up the party everyone. You have 30 seconds – and we're going to need a pianist.

DAME HARI-KIRI: Oh, this is too much!

CLIVE: No time to worry about that now. Needs must as the devil drives, as they say. Necessity is the mother of invention, and all that...

REVEREND: A bird in the hand is worth two blind bats in one basket.

DAME HARI-KIRI, CLIVE and VERITY *look askance at the* REVEREND *as* CELIA *enters DL dusting off her hands.*

CLIVE: (*to F X MANN, unexpectedly determined*) You – down here. And you – (*points to somebody in the front row, apparently at random*) play the piano.

LIGHTING FX: HOUSE LIGHTS DOWN

F X MANN *and* MISS PHILLIMORE *come up from the audience – too bewildered to fight back. During the following announcement and* ALVAR LIDELL's *introduction,* CLIVE *directs* F X MANN *to stand behind the counter and points out various bits of equipment under it and the microphone hanging over it.* DAME HARI-KIRI *escorts* MISS PHILLIMORE *to the piano. Both couples mime (in unison) that neither* FX MANN *nor* MISS PHILIMORE *have scripts or music and that they must make it up as they go along. The 'cast' prepare themselves with their scripts behind the two microphones DS just in time for the introductory bars of* Who Do You Think You Are Kidding, Mr Hitler. *They look surprisingly professional.*

DOTTI: (*over loudspeaker*) Ten seconds to go. There's a short introduction by Alvar Lidell, then you're on your own. (*slight pause*) May your God go with you. Six, five…

ALVAR LIDDEL: (*over loudspeaker, even drunker than before*) Give us the mic' than you old bat!

DOTTI: (*over loudspeaker, flustered*) …two, one. On air.

LIGHTING FX: *The* ON AIR *light comes on*

SOUND FX: *We hear the last few bars of Chattanooga Choo Choo dying away.*

During the following speech, MOLLY PROPPEMUP *peers round the door DL in a very secretive manner. She is searching for the* REVEREND, *spots him and enters as quietly as possible. She is carrying a long feather duster.*

ALVAR LIDELL: *(using his plummy, radio announcer's voice with no hint of drunkenness)* That was Chattanooga Choo-Choo from the Glenn Miller Band, which concludes our short programme of music for this evening. Just starting on the Light Programme is the new quiz series 'What's My Line?' with the young and thrusting Eamon Andrews. Meanwhile, here on the Home Service, we have pleasure in presenting a special seasonal play entitled 'Aladdin A Brown Serge Suit', or 'It's Behind You, Mr. Hitler'.

Towards the end of Alvar Lidell's introduction, MOLLY PROPPEMUP, *who has been edging closer to the* REVEREND *by pretending to dust things (including* DAME HARI-KIRI *and the* BOYS, *positions herself in front of him. When she is quite sure that no-one else is watching her, and with her back to the audience, she opens her housecoat and 'flashes' the* REVEREND. *The* REVEREND *is shocked and stunned.*

SOUND FX: Who Do You Think You Are Kidding, Mr. Hitler (*about 10 seconds only*)

SERGEANT MAJOR BALTHAZAR/REVEREND: (*having to be shaken into action by* DAME HARI-

KIRI *as he is still trying to recover from being 'flashed'*) Sound reveille!

The REVEREND *points to* F X MANN *to indicate that she has to make the sound effect. F X MANN panics, looks wide-eyed, then leans into the microphone and makes a noise roughly approximating to 'reveille' played on a cornet.*

SERGEANT MAJOR BALTHAZAR/REVEREND: Wakey, wakey, rise and shine. It's 5 o'clock. It's another jolly day in the Great British Army and we've got a little war to win today. Get those hairy, skinny, little legs of yours out of bed and onto that parade ground in five minutes or it'll be spud-bashing time for the lot of you from here 'til demob day!

ALADDIN/VERITY: Oh, Sergeant Major, must we get up so early in the morning?

BALTHAZAR/REVEREND: And who are you, boy?

ALADDIN/VERITY: Aladdin, sir.

BALTHAZAR/REVEREND: Aladdin in a brown serge suit – eh? Perhaps you'd like me to bring you a nice cup of tea each morning?

ALADDIN/VERITY: Could you bring me a paper too? I like The People.

BALTHAZAR/REVEREND: Well, I'm one of those people you'd better learn <u>not</u> to like. More cheek from you, my lad, and I'll make your life hell on earth. Aladdin indeed. This army's turning into a proper pantomime.

PRIVATE WISHY/WILLIE: Oh no, it isn't.

BALTHAZAR/REVEREND: Who said that?

WISHY AND WASHY/WILLIE AND DICKIE: (*pointing at each other*) He did, Sir.

BALTHAZAR/REVEREND: That's enough. It's guard duties for the lot of you. Report to me at 18:00 hours. (*makes a 'door closing' sign to F X MANN who responds with the right sound, a big grin and a 'thumbs up'*)

ALADDIN/VERITY: He's a nasty piece of work.

WISHY/WILLIE: You were very cheeky to him though, Aladdin.

ALADDIN/VERITY: So were you, Wishy and Washy.

DAME HARI-KIRI *goes over to* MISS PHILLIMORE *and mimes to her to be ready to play.* MISS PHILLIMORE *starts to panic.*

WASHY/DICKIE: We'll have to be careful. He'll be watching out for us from now on.

WISHY/WILLIE: Let's go down the NAAFI later and see our Mum. She'll know what to do about him.

ALADDIN/VERITY: Okay, we'd better get on parade first though or he'll be dropping us in the glasshouse.

F X MANN *drops a bucket of glass with resounding effect but her smile soon changes when everyone scowls at her. She shrugs her shoulders.* DAME HARI-KIRI *prods* MISS PHILLIMORE, *who plays a short piece of 'fill-in' music to indicate a change of scene. It works well and she beams broadly to* DAME HARI-KIRI.

NARRATOR/CLIVE: (*wearing a top hat*) Later that day, in the NAAFI.

ALADDIN/VERITY: Hello, Widow Twankey.

WIDOW TWANKEY/DAME HARI-KIRI: (*has to be prodded by* VERITY *to come in on cue as she is still busy smiling at* MISS PHILLIMORE) Don't call me that, Aladdin. I'm your Aunty Wanda.

ALADDIN/VERITY: You'll always be Widow Twankey to me, Auntie.

WASHY/DICKIE: Hot teas all round, Mum.

WIDOW TWANKEY/DAME HARI-KIRI: Hello Washy.

F X MANN *starts making 'tea-making' noises with cups and spoons.* MOLLY PROPPEMUP *beckons to the* REVEREND. *He ignores her.*

WISHY/WILLIE: Got any crumpets?

WIDOW TWANKEY/DAME HARI-KIRI: Hello Wishy. Crumpets are off. There's a war on.

ALADDIN/VERITY: Jerry's bombed the bakery again, has he?

F X MANN *starts making loud bubbling noises. The cast look round rather shocked and* F X MANN *mimes pouring water from a kettle.*

WIDOW TWANKEY/DAME HARI-KIRI: *(thinking quickly)* Oh dear – I think the urn's boiled over.

ALADDIN/VERITY: *(improvising)* Oh, what a mess.

WIDOW TWANKEY/DAME HARI-KIRI: *(more improvising)* I'll mop it up.

F X MANN: *(enjoying getting in to her 'part' and oblivious to the havoc she is causing)* Slosh, slosh, slosh.

CLIVE *and the* REVEREND *hunt through their scripts. They are lost!* DAME HARI-KIRI *mimes to* F X MANN *to be quiet. Her shoulders slump and she looks decidedly grumpy.*

WIDOW TWANKEY/DAME HARI-KIRI: *(getting back to the script)* So – you're all in the guardhouse, are you?

CLIVE *and the* REVEREND *find their places in the script again with great relief.* MOLLY PROPPEMUP *beckons to* REVEREND *again. This time he takes the hint and tries to edge towards* MOLLY *without being too obvious about it.*

WISHY/WILLIE: It's that horrid Sergeant Major Balthazar.

WASHY/DICKIE: He's got it in for us.

ALADDIN/VERITY: It wouldn't surprise me if he was secretly a German spy. I can't believe that such a nasty man could be on our side.

BALTHAZAR/REVEREND: (*having to return to his microphone very quickly to get his line in*) What's this, what's this? Rebellion in the ranks?

WIDOW TWANKEY/DAME HARI-KIRI: Not at all, Sergeant Major. We were talking about someone entirely different. Not you at all. Doesn't even look like you.

BALTHAZAR/REVEREND: Good. After all, I'm sure we can all be friends.

WISHY AND WASHY/WILLIE AND DICKIE: (*together*) Friends?!

DAME HARI-KIRI *gives* MISS PHILLIMORE *a prod and she plays another few bars of incidental music to indicate a scene change.*

LIGHTING FX: ON AIR *light goes off*

DOTTI: (*over loudspeaker*) Keep it up, everyone. You're doing marvellously. (*pause*) Cue the narrator.

LIGHTING FX: ON AIR *light goes on*

MISS PHILLIMORE *stops playing*

NARRATOR/CLIVE: (*in top hat*) Later – in the guardhouse...

ALADDIN/VERITY: Goodness gracious, my toes are cold.

WISHY/WILLIE: Stamp your feet. You'll feel warmer.

F X MANN *stamps a pair of boots up and down in a grit tray*

WASHY/DICKIE: Walk up and down. Get your circulation going.

F X MANN *makes 'walking up and down noises with boots and grit tray*

WISHY/WILLIE: (*seeing an opportunity to have some fun at F X MANN's expense*) Let's all do a quick foxtrot, then run round the barracks for 10 minutes. We'll all feel much better then.

F X MANN *responds as best she can*

ALADDIN/VERITY: (*putting her hand over microphone, sotto, to* WISHY)   That's not in the script. Stop messing about.

VERITY *waves to* F X MANN *to stop the 'running' noises. From behind, the* REVEREND *clips* WILLIE *round the ear.* DAME HARI-KIRI *sees this, glares at the* REVEREND *and comforts* WILLIE

WISHY/WILLIE: Ow!

ALADDIN/VERITY: (*improvising*)   Oh dear, Wishy, did you trip over on the nasty gravel? Perhaps we'd better stop.

F X MANN *stops making 'running' noises.* CLIVE *looks aghast. He cannot follow the script.*

ALADDIN/VERITY: (*points to the line in* CLIVE's *script*)   Halt! Who goes there?

COLONEL'S DAUGHTER/CLIVE: (*relieved, put's on a blonde wig with a tiara in it. In a very high pitched voice*) It is only me – the Colonel's daughter.

ALADDIN/VERITY: Are you friend or foe?

COLONEL'S DAUGHTER/CLIVE: I'm very friendly.

WASHY/DICKIE: Ooooh!....

COLONEL'S DAUGHTER/CLIVE: Can I come into your nice, warm guardhouse. It's frightfully cold out here.

WISHY/WILLIE: Oooooooh!....

ALADDIN/VERITY: Of course you may. I could not bear to think of you shivering alone out there. Come inside and warm yourself at our hot coals.

F X MANN *makes a 'door shutting' noise*

NARRATOR/CLIVE: (*in top hat*) And so, the seeds of true love are sown in a chance meeting by the guardhouse gate.

MISS PHILLIMORE *plays a short burst of incidental music. The two* BOYS *take the opportunity during the next scene to creep behind the* REVEREND. DICKIE *loads a pea-shooter with pieces of paper and takes pot shots at him while* WILLIE *blows into a brown paper bag and creeps up close.*

COLONEL/CLIVE: (*in army officer's hat and a very gruff voice*) What was she doing by the guardhouse gate? That's what I want to know?

COLONEL'S WIFE/CLIVE: (*in a lady's hat and 'Colonel's wife' voice*) I expect she was just out for a stroll, my dear. I'm sure our dear darling daughter would not be up to any mischief.

COLONEL/CLIVE: (*army hat, CLIVE searches through the script to see if anyone else is going to help him with this scene*) Out for a stroll? At one o'clock in the morning?! At five degrees below zero?! In an army barracks?!!

COLONEL'S WIFE/CLIVE: (*lady's hat*)   She's a very hardy girl.

COLONEL/CLIVE: (*army hat*)   She'd need to be…

WILLIE *bursts his paper bag next to the* REVEREND'S *ear. He jumps out of his skin and his 'secret document' falls to the floor.* MOLLY PROPPEMUP *sees an opportunity to grab the document but is too slow and* WILLIE *gets it first.*

CLIVE: (*own voice*)   …What on earth!

ALADDIN/VERITY: (*quick-witted as usual*)   It was a one-gun salute, Colonel. In honour of your -

COLONEL/CLIVE: (*army hat, interested to know how* VERITY *is going to get them out of this one*) Yes?

ALADDIN/VERITY: - your daughter's engagement!

COLONEL/CLIVE: (*army hat*)   What?!!

COLONEL'S WIFE/CLIVE: (*lady's hat*)   Oh, how marvellous.

ALADDIN/VERITY: To me. Private Aladdin.

COLONEL'S DAUGHTER/CLIVE: (*blond wig and tiara*) Isn't that wonderful, Daddy?

COLONEL'S WIFE/CLIVE: (*lady's hat*)   I'm so happy.

COLONEL/CLIVE: (*army hat*)   Over my dead body!

MISS PHILLIMORE *plays a loud and sinister burst on the piano.* CLIVE *faints with exhaustion.* DAME HARI-KIRI *fans him with her fox fur. The* REVEREND *has recovered enough to clip both the* BOYS *round the ear gain and wrenches his 'secret document' from* WILLIE's *grasp. He raises it aloft as if to beat* WILLIE *over the head with it and* MOLLY PROPPEMUP *vainly tries to jump at it from behind him, but she is too short.*

NARRATOR/ALADDIN/VERITY: (*standing in as narrator while* CLIVE *is unconscious and trying to get the radio play back on track*) Later, back in the guardhouse... (*she beckons to the* REVEREND *who has to find his place in the script*)

BALTHAZAR/REVEREND: So, Aladdin. You've got yourself engaged to the Colonel's daughter.

ALADDIN/VERITY: Yes, I have Sargent-Major Balthazar. We're going to be married and live happily ever after. We may be poor but we are pure and honest and -

BALTHAZAR/REVEREND: Oh, shut up. The only way you'll ever be able to marry the Colonel's daughter is to get on the right side of the Colonel.

ALADDIN/VERITY: But how shall I do that? He seems to be rather ill-disposed towards me.

BALTHAZAR/REVEREND: He thinks you're the most idle little layabout he's ever clapped eyes on and he'd like to see you boiled, chopped up into little pieces and fed to the fishes. If you get within so much as a mile of his daughter he'll have you cleaning tanks with your toothbrush for the duration.

ALADDIN/VERITY: He doesn't like me, then?

BALTHAZAR/REVEREND: He will do.

ALADDIN/VERITY: But how?

BALTHAZAR/REVEREND: (*conspiratorially*) I've got a little proposition for you; which you might find to your advantage. Follow me.

MISS PHILLIMORE *plays a few bars of 'The Sugar Plum Fairy'.* CLIVE *comes to and is shown where they are in the script by* DAME HARI-KIRI.

ALADDIN/VERITY: But, Sergeant Major, this is the Army Headquarters' secret underground bunker. We should not be here.

BALTHAZAR/REVEREND: Keep your noise down.

ALADDIN/VERITY: Are you sure the Colonel has asked you to retrieve this lost document?

BALTHAZAR/REVEREND: Do you want everyone to hear you? Just squeeze through this gap, find the secret - I mean, the <u>lost</u> document, and pass it up to me.

ALADDIN/VERITY: I feel quite positive that the Colonel would find more conventional means of retrieving his own property. Why does he not simply ask the storekeeper to search for it in the morning?

BALTHAZAR/REVEREND: Because the storekeeper wouldn't know what to look for.

ALADDIN/VERITY: But you said it was simply a laundry list that had been mislaid.

BALTHAZAR/REVEREND: Well, it was written on the back of something else.

ALADDIN/VERITY: What?

BALTHAZAR/REVEREND: Just some old (*mumbling*) Allied Invasion Plans.

ALADDIN/VERITY: Old ones?

BALTHAZAR/REVEREND: Of course. Very old, redundant, no use to anybody any more. Would I lie to you?

ALADDIN/VERITY: Well – I don't know….

BALTHAZAR/REVEREND: Get yourself down there boy – right now – or I'll have you scrubbing the mess room floor for a month!

ALADDIN/VERITY: And if I do find the – laundry list – what then?

BALTHAZAR/REVEREND: You give it to me. I give it to the Colonel. He gets promoted to General. He makes me a Captain and you get to take his daughter's hand in marriage.

ALADDIN/VERITY: It must be a very important laundry list.

BALTHAZAR/REEREND: They're his very best 'parading about in' clothes and he wants to get them back from the laundry.

ALADIN/VERITY: Oh well. Do I go through here?

BALTHAZAR/REVEREND: (*eagerly*) Yes, yes.

ALADDIN/VERITY: Her hand in marriage you say.

BALTHAZAR/REEREND: Maybe some other bits as well. Now hurry up!

ALADDIN/VERITY: It's a bit of a squeeze.

BALTHAZAR/REVEREND: That's why it's a job for a scrawny little – small boned person like yourself.

ALADDIN/VERITY: I'm nearly there. One last push!

F X MANN *pulls the cork from a bottle.*

ALADDIN/VERITY: I'm through.

BALTHAZAR/REEREND: Search through the papers over there. It's marked TOP SECRET.

ALADDIN/VERITY: (*sees the 'secret document' in the REVEREND's back pocket and for dramatic effect pulls it out and brandishes it above her head*) I have it!

BALTHAZAR/REVEREND: (*shocked at losing his document, he reaches out for it desperately*) Then give it to me!

ALADDIN/VERITY: (*holding the document aloft*) First you must promise me that the document is harmless and that I will gain the hand of the Colonel's daughter.

BALTHAZAR/REVEREND: I promise – I promise (*as the* REVEREND) Give it here you little brat. (*The* REVEREND *snatches it from* VERITY *and holds it at arm's length away from her*) Take that! (*with his other hand he crowns* VERITY *over the head with his script*)

F X MANN *makes the sound of someone being hit.* DAME HARI-KIRI, *who was standing behind the* REVEREND, *thinks she is supposed to take the secret document, which she does.*

REVEREND: (*all pretence of acting as the Sergeant Major has gone*) ...and that...and that...and that...and that!

With each 'and that' the REVEREND *beats* VERITY *over the head with his script and the document gets passed from hand to hand along a line from* DAME HARI-KIRI *to* CLIVE *to* WILLIE *to* DICKIE *and finally to* MOLLY PROPPEMUP, *who is standing in front of the piano. Each pass/hit is accompanied by* F X MANN *making the sound of someone being hit.* MOLLY PROPPEMUP *breathes a long sigh of relief and opens her housecoat to reveal a German uniform underneath. She secretes the secret document in her bosom. From now on* MOLLY PROPPEMUP *tries to get away from the scene but there are too many people in the way and she keeps getting accosted by the two* BOYS *who ply her with various black market items.*

There is a slight pause while everyone catches their breath.

VERITY: (*sotto to* REVEREND) Was that in the script?

REVEREND: I'm sorry, I got carried away.

LIGHTING FX: ON AIR *light goes off*

DOTTI DARLING: (*over loudspeaker*) Cue music. (*Over the following speech,* DAME HARI-KIRI *rushes to the piano, getting in* MOLLY PROPPEMUP's *way and* *forcing her back to the front of the piano. She nudges* MISS PHILLIMORE *and props up music in front of her.* MISS PHILLMORE *starts playing The Dance of the Sugar Plum Fairy again.)* You're doing fine. Try to keep a little closer to the script, darlings, if you can. But don't worry. Nobody will have noticed anything wrong.

LIGHTING FX: ON AIR *light goes on*

NARRATOR/CLIVE: (*in top hat*) ...and so, Aladdin finds himself alone and friendless deep underground. (MISS PHILLIMORE *stops playing*) The air is filled with strange noises.

F X MANN *looks shocked. She reaches for the nearest thing to hand, a salad spinner, and makes a sound like an underground train.* ALL THE CAST *look at her. She shrugs.*

F X MANN: Mind the gap.

ALADDIN/VERITY: (*trying to retrieve the situation*) Oh dear, I must have been down here so long that I'm having hallucinations. I'm sure that couldn't really have been an underground train. I must try to keep alert. (*points straight ahead, mimicking a 'your country needs you' poster*) Be alert! Britain Needs

> Lerts! (*pause*) Hello, what's this? It looks a bit like a grenade. It's very dirty though. I wonder what would happen if I just give it a little shine? After all, just because there's a war on, we don't have to lose all sense of propriety. A little spit and polish wouldn't hurt it, I'm sure.

F X MANN *makes polishing sounds with a chamois leather and a pane of glass.*

ALADDIN/VERITY: (*continuing*) Goodness, it's ever so dirty. I don't suppose anyone has polished this grenade in months.

From the back of the studio there is a loud bang, a flash and a cloud of smoke as F X MANN *sets off a flash box. She looks smug as the rest of the cast (and probably the audience as well) reel from the shock.* DAME HARI-KIRI *almost faints.* CELIA STRINGBAG *waves a handkerchief over her face to revive her.*

ALADDIN/VERITY: (*the first to recover her composure*) Golly gosh – my grenade must have gone off pop.

GENIE/CLIVE: (*in Chinese 'coolie' hat*) Not at all, Aladdin. It is I.

DAME HARI-KIRI *mimes that she needs a drink.* CELIA STRINGBAG *exits DL. The two* BOYS *corner* MOLLY PROPPEMUP *by the piano.* DICKIE *secretively pulls up one of his sleeves to display an armful of watches.* MOLLY *mimes that she is not interested but cannot get away. During the next few pages the two* BOYS *pull out an incredible array of different black market goods (nylons, purses, handkerchiefs, scarves etc.) none of which* MOLLY *can be persuaded to buy.*

ALADDIN/VERITY: Who's there?

GENIE/CLIVE: *(coolie hat)* I am your genie.

ALADDIN/VERITY: The genie of the lamp?

GENIE/CLIVE: *(coolie hat)* No, no. That's my bigger and much uglier cousin. I am the Genie with the Light Brown Hair.

ALADDIN/VERITY: I have heard of you. But how did you get down here?

GENIE/CLIVE: *(coolie hat)* I was trapped inside your grenade by an evil munitions packer from *(next door village or location)*. When you polished it, I was released from my magic prison. Now I am yours to serve and obey. (CLIVE *bows*)

ALADDIN/VERITY: That's jolly nice of you. What do you do, exactly?

GENIE/CLIVE: *(coolie hat)* I grant wishes. Your wish is my command, oh Master. *(he bows)*

ALADDIN/VERITY: Gosh, this is spiffing fun. Do you mean I can wish for anything?

GENIE/CLIVE: *(coolie hat)* Anything at all.

ALADDIN/VERITY: Can you make England win the next Test Series?

GENIE/CLIVE: *(coolie hat)* Be reasonable.

ALADDIN/VERITY: Can you get us out of here?

GENIE/CLIVE: *(coolie hat)* As easy as winking. Where would you like to go?

ALADDIN/VERITY: Into the arms of my sweetheart, the Colonel's daughter.

GENIE/CLIVE: *(coolie hat)* Close your eyes (*raises his hands in a dramatic gesture*) Take us to the place Aladdin loves best/Tucked up close to his sweetheart's – chest.

MISS PHILLIMORE *plays some suitable incidental music to register their transportation.* CELIA STRINGBAG *enters DL with a small tray with a green cocktail on it.*

ALADDIN/VERITY: Oo-er, I'm feeling all queasy.

GENIE/CLIVE: *(coolie hat)* It's always like that the first time. Hold on to your hat. We're coming in to land!

COLONEL'S DAUGHTER/CLIVE: *(blond wig and tiara)* Ow! Oooh, Aladdin, where did you come from? And where do you think you're going?

ALADDIN/VERITY: I was transported here by a friendly genie.

GENIE/CLIVE: *(coolie hat)* ...with light brown hair. (*he steals the drink from* CELIA's *tray as she walks past and gulps it down.* CELIA *exits DL again in a huff*)

ALADDIN/VERITY: ...with light brown hair. He will grant me anything I wish...

GENIE/CLIVE: *(coolie hat)* ...any three things you wish – oh, Master.

ALADDIN/VERITY: ...any <u>three</u> things I wish. You didn't tell me that.

GENIE/CLIVE: *(coolie hat)* Sorry – must have forgotten.

ALADDIN/VERITY: Anyway – I was in this underground bunker....

F X MANN *starts the salad spinner again but* ALL THE CAST *glare at her and she stops immediately with an apologetic smile.*

ALADDIN/VERITY: Sergeant Major Balthazar wanted me to get him something. It was for your father actually. – a laundry list.

COLONEL'S DAUGHTER/CLIVE: *(blond wig and tiara)* A laundry list? That doesn't sound...

ALADDIN/VERITY: It was written on the back of some old secret document, I think. Nothing important.

CELIA STRINGBAG *enters DL again with another green cocktail on her tray. During the following speeches she makes wide berth of* CLIVE *to avoid the drink being stolen again.*

COLONEL'S DAUGHTER/CLIVE: *(blond wig and tiara)* Nothing very important?! A secret document from the underground bunker? I bet that was the radio call signs for the Allied Invasion Plan. Daddy's always talking about them in his sleep. This could be the end of the war for us all!

ALADDIN/VERITY: Oh, jolly good. I wasn't enjoying it very much anyway.

COLONEL'S DAUGHTER/CLIVE: *(blond wig and tiara)* You idiot, Aladdin. We must get the secret document back from the Sergeant Major and avert a national disaster. If we don't, we could all be speaking German by the end of the month.

ALADDIN/VERITY: But how are we going to do that?

GENIE/CLIVE: *(coolie hat)* Can I be of assistance?

ALADDIN/VERITY: I wish my Auntie Wanda was here. She'd know what to do.

GENIE/ALADDIN: *(coolie hat)* Your wish is my command, oh Master.

Just as CELIA STRINGBAG reaches DAME HARI-KIRI with her drink, there is another 'flash' from the rear of the hall. CELIA jumps with fright and pours the drink all over herself. She stomps off DL in another huff.

WIDOW TWANKEY/DAME HARI-KIRI: Oh, my corns and blisters! What happened then? Where am I?

COLONEL'S DAUGHTER/CLIVE: *(blond wig and tiara)* You twit, Aladdin. You've wasted one of your wishes.

ALADDIN/VERITY: We wished you here, Widow Twankey and my Genie made it come true.

WIDOW TWANKEY/DAME HARI-KIRI: You've been on the gin again, haven't you, Aladdin?

COLONEL'S DAUGHTER/CLIVE: *(blond wig and tiara)* We have to hurry. Sergeant Major Balthazar has stolen a very important secret document, and we have to get it back before he can pass it on to a German spy.

WIDOW TWANKEY/DAME HARI-KIRI: The Sergeant Major, eh? I knew there was something funny about him when he asked for Wienerschnitzel with his mash and beans.

ALADDIN/VERITY: Look – there he goes!

F X MANN *makes walking noises*

COLONEL'S DAUGHTER/CLIVE: *(blond wig and tiara)* Don't let him get away!

WIDOW TWANKEY/DAME HARI-KIRI: After him!

F X MANN *makes running noises*

ALADDIN/VERITY: Faster – faster – he's getting away!

F X MANN *speeds up*

WIDOW TWANKEY/DAME HARI-KIRI: I can't keep up. Somebody call me a taxi!

ALADDIN/VERITY: You're a taxi!

SOUND FX: *We hear the sound of a car pulling up with a squeal of brakes*

NARRATOR/CLIVE: *top hat)* And so, they all piled into the back of Widow Twankey and soon caught up with the wicked double-agent. *(raises his fist in the air and tries to coax a big cheer from the audience)*

ALADDIN/VERITY: Gotcha – you dastardly cad!

BALTHAZAR/REVEREND: Ow – oooh – ouch! You're twisting my arm!

ALADDIN/VERITY: There's more where that came from, you villain. What have you done with the secret document?

BALTHAZAR/REVEREND: You're too late. I've already passed it on to my contact, the brilliant German Spy, Helga von Bratwurst - ?.....(*the* REVEREND *tails off as he recognises the name he has just read out*)

MOLLY PROPPEMUP *squeals when she hears the* REVEREND *using her real name.* DICKIE *is in the process of pulling out a length of sausages from down his trousers. They are black market sausages that he is trying to sell to* MOLLY PROPPEMUP. DAME HARI-KIRI *turns round and misinterprets* MOLLY's *scream, sees the sausages and screams herself. She clips* DICKIE *round the ear and drags him off to a corner where she tells him off.*

VERITY: *(not Aladdin any longer)* Yes, Reverend Cadwallader-Trump – Helga von Bratwurst!

REVEREND: You mean...?

VERITY: Yes, you evil bounder. We were on to your game all along. This whole charade has been played out just to catch the pair of you.

CLIVE: *(searching through his script)* What's going on? Where are we?

DAME HARI-KIRI: *(also searching through her script)* I don't know. I'm lost.

VERITY: This is <u>not</u> the Reverend Reginald Cadwallader-Trump, and he is <u>not</u> here to do The Epilogue. *(to REVEREND)* It was a fair stab at a disguise Herr Trumpenblaster, but no self-respecting English vicar would wear a summer jacket and a Panama hat on Christmas Eve.

DAME HARI-KIRI, CELIA STRINGBAG, F X MANN *and* MISS PHILLIMORE *gasp in unison.*

VERITY: *(pointing to* MOLLY*)* And as for you.

CLIVE: What?

VERITY: She is not Molly Proppemup, the slightly odd but harmless BBC char lady she seems to be.

MOLLY PROPPEMUP *proudly takes off her housecoat to reveal her German uniform. She takes the secret document from down her bosom and brandishes it triumphantly.*

VERITY: She is Helga von Bratwurst, the well-known German spy and mistress of disguise.

DAME HARI-KIRI, CELIA STRINGBAG, F X MANN *and* MISS PHILLIMORE *gasp in unison.* MOLLY PROPPEMUP *struggles to get past the two* BOYS *but they catch her and tie her hands together with the string of sausages. The secret document is passed to* VERITY. *The* REVEREND *starts edging away from the rest of the group.*

DAME HARI-KIRI: And you?

VERITY: I'm sorry – Official Secrets Act and all that...

REVEREND: *(he has reached the exit DR and pulls out a gun)* Bond – Jane Bond – Secret British Agent. Well, Bond, I may be shaken but I'm not stirred. You'll never take me alive. *(he fires)*

LIGHTING FX: BLACKOUT

There is a general melee in the darkness. DAME HARI-KIRI *screams.*

VERITY: Don't let him get away!

WILLIE: Yahoo!

In the darkness VERITY, CLIVE, *the two* BOYS, MOLLY PROPPEMUP, MISS PHILLIMORE *and* F X MANN *all exit DL. There is a pause.*

LIGHTING FX:	ON AIR light goes off
DOTTI: *(over loudspeaker)*	Is everything all right out there? I seem to be a bit lost in the script, loveys. It all seemed to get a bit confused towards the end, but I'm sure you're doing very well. Nobody notices if a few lines go astray, you know. *(pause)* Is there anybody there?
LIGHTING FX:	*The* LIGHTS COME UP SLOWLY

DAME HARI-KIRI *is seated at the piano stool. She is wearing one of Clive's hats at an impossible angle and her hands have been tied with the sausages.* CELIA STRINGBAG *is feeding her sips of cocktail and is gently singing her a lullaby. The* DAME *looks very faraway and faint.*

DAME HARI-KIRI:	I'll never sing again you know. What will my public think of my now? *(she bursts into tears)*

The door DL bursts open and SIMONE deWITT *enters looking very flustered*

SIMONE:	Now then, is everybody ready to start?
LIGHTING FX:	BLACKOUT
SOUND FX:	*A few bars of Who Do You Think You Are Kidding, Mr. Hitler? Is heard over the loudspeaker, followed by*

Glenn Miller's Little Brown Jug which plays softly in the background while the cast come on to take their bows with the following voiceover

ALVAR LIDELL: (*over loudspeaker*) You have been listening to, and watching, There Will Be Some Slight Interference. Our cast for tonight were...

Actor's name as Miss Phillimore, a passing pianist...

Actor's name as F X Mann, a sound technician of unsound mind...

Actor's name a Dotti Darling, the unflappable BBC producer. Thank you lovey...

Actor's name as Simone deWitt. Simone was a volunteer floor manager for the BBC. Unfortunately, she couldn't get a job packing parachutes for the enemy, or we might have won the war a little sooner...

Actors' names played Willie and Dickie 'the Dip' Nobbs. *Actors' names* will next be seen appearing in 'It Wasn't Me, Governor' for the

Prisoners' Theatre Guild, Wormwood Scrubs...

Actor's name as Celia Stringbag, constant companion, personal dresser and thorn in the side of Dame Hari-Kiri...

Actor's name played Dame Hari-Kiri de Kanawerms and Widow Twankey. Once Britain's greatest opera singer, she is now reduced to entertaining the boys from the back of a troop carrier. Sometimes she even keeps her clothes on.

Actor's name as Molly Proppemup, the BBC char lady who was really Helga von Bratwurst the infamous German Spy and mistress of disguise...

Actor's name was Clive Prendaghast, a man of many parts, but few in working order. *Actor's name* also played the Colonel, the Colonel's Wife, the Colonel's Daughter. The Narrator and the Genie with the Light Brown Hair. Confused? He is...

Actor's name played the Reverend Reginald Cadwallader-Trump, who pretended to be Sergeant Major Balthazar but was really Herr Trumpenblaster, the evil double agent. Boo – hiss...

And, of course, *Actor's name*, who nobly played Jane Bond nobly playing Verity Pureheart who was nobly playing Private Aladdin...

And lastly, the voice of the BBC, Alvar Lidell. (*actor enters DL. All bow*)

CURTAIN

Printed in Great Britain
by Amazon